# *A Beginner's Guide to:*
# MINDFULNESS

## MARION McGEOUGH

© Marion McGeough all rights reserved

All rights reserved. This book may not be reproduced, transmitted, or stored in whole or in part by any means including graphic, electronic or mechanical without expressed written consent of the publisher/author except in the case of brief quotations embodied in critical articles and reviews. The right of Marion McGeough to be identified as the author/owner of this work has been asserted by them in accordance with the Copyright, Designs and Patents Act 1988.

Published by Marion McGeough.

All rights reserved. No part of this publication may be reproduced, stored in a retrieval system or transmitted in any form or by any means, electronic, mechanical, photocopying, recording or otherwise without the prior permission of the publisher.

While the publisher has taken reasonable care in the preparation of this book, the publisher makes no representation, express or implied, with regard to the accuracy of the information contained in this book and cannot accept legal responsibility or liability for any errors or omissions from the book or the consequences thereof.

Products or services that are referred to in this book may be either trademarks and/or registered trademarks of their respective owners. The publisher and author make no claims to these trademarks.

A CIP Catalogue record for this book is available from the British Library.

Formatting and cover design by ebook-designs.co.uk

This is a work of fiction. The events and characters described herein are imaginary and are not intended to refer to specific places or living persons. The opinions expressed in this manuscript are solely the

opinions of the author.

# CHAPTER 1: WHAT IS MINDFULNESS?

**The word mindful has become very popular in recent times. I recently received an email requesting that I become "mindful" of a person's current situation. In this context, "being mindful" really meant to tell me to be careful. Be careful of what you say to a particular person, the email was telling me, because they have had a recent bereavement. However, this is not really what mindfulness truly is and how the word should be used.**

So, what is mindfulness? Mindfulness, in a nutshell, is about living in the present. Now you may be thinking, is that it? Is that what all of the fuss is about? All I have to do is live day to day. Well, not really. This is because, as with most things, once you begin to have an understanding of something there is usually a lot more to it than meets the eye.

If I can just go back to the part of mindfulness that you understand so far: the living in the present part. How many of us really do that? Just stop what you are doing for a minute and think about this. Take eating as a simple example. Many of us do other things when we eat. We might read a newspaper, watch TV, talk to other people, eat whilst driving or even eat in between getting ready to go to work. Whilst you are eating and doing something else your mind is also elsewhere. You are not living in the moment. Your mind is either in the past or the future. Now, going back to eating, this is one of the reasons why some of us are overweight. We do not realise how much food we are eating because we are not paying attention to the food that is going into our mouths. Not only are we not paying attention, we are not really enjoying what we are eating. We are not allowing our taste buds to really taste and for us to become satisfied. In order to really understand what I mean try this exercise:

Think of your favourite, naughty indulgent food. For many people this is chocolate. Go and get a piece of chocolate, or a chocolate cookie, or whatever you have in your cupboard at the moment. If you don't like chocolate, are allergic to it, or you would simply prefer to choose something else then go ahead and do so.

Eat your chosen food whilst reading the newspaper or an article that holds your interest online.

Note down how it felt to eat that food.

Now, go and get another cookie, piece of chocolate, or whatever you want to eat for the purpose of this exercise. Now eat the food without any distractions. Just sit there and chew the food without reading, talking, answering text messages/email or anything else.

Note down what it felt like when you were eating.

My guess is that when you were carrying out the second part of the exercise you paid attention to what you were doing. You may have been able to describe the food that you were eating in greater detail. This may have included the texture, how it really tasted, what it felt like and how it felt when you swallowed what you were eating. You most likely felt more satisfied eating in this way.

Now that you are beginning to get some idea of what mindfulness is I want you to take a few moments to look at your day to day life. Most of us live in a hectic, frantic world. The majority of us have loads of gadgets and devices at home which were devised to make life easier. Great, this allows us to have more time. The sad thing is, what do the majority of us do with the extra free time? We simply fill it up with more work or work related tasks. Is that what you do? We do not use this time to pursue hobbies and interests but instead most of us are engaged in activities which add rather than reduce our level of stress, anxiety or depression. To make matters even worse, the majority of things that most of us do are boring, mindless tasks.

In fact, if an alien spaceship were to come and land on the earth and a number of aliens were to observe human behaviour I am sure that they would be truly amazed at how we humans in the West can live in our own prison. It is a prison that we build ourselves and only we ourselves have the key and we CAN open the door. However, the sad thing is that many of us do not even realise this. We live our lives in our own prison of perception.

I am sure that you are reading this book as there is something that you want to change in your life. For many it is simply that they want to feel better about themselves, they simply want to feel joyful and happy again. They want to feel positive emotions instead of, well not really feeling anything. This book does not promise that you will feel happy and joyful for the rest of your life. That would be a ridiculous and wrong promise to make. Life is full of up's and down's and it is dangerous to believe that one will not or should not experience some sadness and grief from time to time. Instead, this book will show you how you can train your mind to think and look at things differently.

Many of us train our bodies and find that the discipline of a structured and challenging exercise programme has many rewards beyond the obvious benefits of improved physical health. Few of us have learnt how to train our minds. We may think that we have control over our minds but the sad truth is that few of us truly have this ability. Begin to discipline your mind now. You may be surprised at what you discover.

# CHAPTER 2: OUR MODERN LIVES

**I**f we observe a baby, and yes, we were all babies at one time, we notice that a baby truly lives in the moment. A baby will cry when it is hungry, cold, wants attention, wants a nappy change and for a thousand other reasons.

If you watch children in a playground during school time, for them life is very simple. When playing a game the children become very absorbed with the game that they are playing. Perhaps one of the children becomes a leader and assigns a role to each of the others. Each child knows what is expected of them and the game flows smoothly until something goes wrong and perhaps one of the children ends up crying. An adult then comes along and the game ends as the children go back to the classroom. The child that has been upset is comforted and told that everything will be okay. A short while after the children have been back in class the teacher introduces a topic which is of great interest. The children forget about what has happened in the playground. They become totally absorbed in what is happening at that moment. Generally children like babies live in the moment. So, why are adults so very different? When do we begin to change?

As children go through school their progress, performance and achievements are monitored by tests in one form or the other. Children seem to have very little time to become creative, to take part in physical exercise so that they can blow off some steam. Very often even the simple walk to school has been replaced by the car. I remember walking to school each and every day. I would meet up with friends and we would spend the half hour walking to school gossiping, giggling and bonding.

A few years later, when the child has developed into a young adult and enters the workplace a great deal of apprehension, excitement and even fear begins to take hold. For some people they begin to think:

- Am I really good enough to do this job?

- What will happen if I do something wrong?

- My colleague is much better at this job than I am.

- I really hate this job but I have a mortgage/bills/car loan to pay so I have to stick with it.

Now that the young adult has a job he or she begins to realise that any negative thoughts and especially any self-doubt must be kept to oneself. They realise that if those negative thoughts are made public they may be used against them. Perhaps they have confided in a colleague at some stage and they have later found out that the colleague that they trusted had gossiped behind their back. This is hurtful and the young adult begins to see the world in a different way. Sure, a child also quickly learns that not everyone can be trusted and not all people are considered kind and good and unfortunately some children experience more of this than others. However, as an adult there is more at stake: family and friends have expectations of you; there may be dependents to provide for. Your boss tells you that reaching targets, maximizing efficiency and the careful use of resources are what is important. In addition, there is always the constant threat that if you do not or cannot achieve what is expected of you, well, there are many who would gladly step in your shoes.

So, what happens next?

Read the story of Amanda below:

Amanda is 42 years old. She is married to Steve, an engineer. Amanda is a graphic designer, self-employed and working from home. Steve often works overseas for several weeks at a time before returning home. Amanda sometimes wishes that she could go with him but this is impossible. Not only do they have two boys, Adam aged 7 and Craig aged 11 who of course need to attend school, Amanda also has elderly parents who needed looking after. Amanda's father has a heart condition and her mother has rheumatoid arthritis in nearly all of her joints. Naturally, these significant health problems prevented Amanda's parents from tending to the garden and looking after the home properly.

Before Amanda became self-employed she had worked as part of a small team in a family run organisation. Amanda had loved the job. She was naturally very creative and she found her job interesting, challenging and enjoyable. Amanda had decided to quit her job after the children were born. She had wanted to be a stay at home mom but she found that if she was honest with herself, she was a little bored.

Steve had been very supportive when she suggested that she become self-employed. Amanda found that her business grew quickly. There was more than enough to keep her busy in between carrying out the chores and looking after the home. With the children both at school Amanda found that initially there was some structure to her day as she was able to drop the boys off at school and work during the school hours.

When her parents became less independent Amanda found that she had to take either one or the other to various hospital appointments. She also had to take her mother shopping and help look after her parent's home. Amanda found that she had less and less time available to do her actual job. Life was becoming a juggling act between looking after her own home, taking and collecting the boys from and to school and various clubs and activities that they were involved with, as well as looking after her parents and doing the actual work that people were paying her for.

Amanda began to think how best to organise her day. She began to get up in the morning an hour before the boys so that she could fit in some work before taking them to school. In addition Amanda worked late into the evening and at weekends .However, Amanda found that she was constantly running around doing things but she seemed to get very little done. When Steve was home Amanda had little time for him as she still had to her own work to do. This often resulted in arguments and they began to grow apart.

One day Amanda received an invitation in the post to a school reunion. She really did not have the time to go but when she received a phone call from an old school friend she was persuaded to change her mind.

As the day approached Amanda really wished that she had declined the invitation but she really could not back out now. Her old friend Becky was looking forward to going and, as they would both be attending together, Amanda really did not have the heart to let her friend down.

Amanda had a great time at the reunion however, she was surprised at how jaded and tired most of her friends looked. When she sat in the taxi on the way home after dropping Becky off her mind began to wander. Amanda began to ask herself questions:

- Why do I feel so tired and stressed out all of the time?

- Is there something wrong with me?

- Why can't I just do things like I used to?

- Why do I feel so empty?

Amanda continued to ask herself searching questions as she paid the taxi driver. She continued to ask herself questions as she paid the babysitter and when she checked on the boys, who were fast asleep, tucked up in their beds. As Amanda herself got ready for bed she made a decision: she was going to get to the bottom of why she was feeling like this. She was a strong woman and she was prepared to make any changes necessary just so that she would feel "normal" again, whatever normal was. And so she pondered the definition of normality as she fell asleep.

After much research Amanda came across the concept of Mindfulness, it changed her life. Are you willing to begin to practice Mindfulness so that you can make the changes that are important to you?

# CHAPTER 3: YOUR EMOTIONS

**If you are like Amanda you may have tried to figure out why you feel a certain way. Well, let me tell you, this is often the wrong thing to do. You may be wondering why this is. Let me take you through this exercise and you will soon find out for yourself:**

**Exercise**

- Think of a problem.

- Spend 5 minutes thinking about this problem.

- Now write down your thoughts and feelings

- And return to this book.

- Now how do you feel?

There is a chance that you may have come to a solution to your problem. This is especially the case if the problem was not really too difficult to solve, or if it simply required technical knowledge as you may have called a friend or consulted a manual. If your problem is one that involves other people you might well have not resolved it. Going back to the question:

"How do you feel?"

My guess is that you feel even worse. You may be more confused, similar problems may have entered your mind. You may feel a bit low, a bit tired and I bet at the back of your mind you are still thinking about the problem that I asked you to think about. If I ask you to stop you will now find it difficult. If you don't believe me try it and see for yourself. Okay, now:

STOP THINKING ABOUT YOUR PROBLEM!

Have you done it?

No, of course not; the more you stop trying to do something the more you want to do it. This is why diets don't work for very long. You tell yourself in a stern, grownup voice that you must NEVER, EVER, EAT CHOCOLATE CAKE AGAIN. And what do you want to do a few seconds or a short time later? You really, really want to eat chocolate in some form or other.

Now there is no point in trying to get angry with yourself and calling yourself a failure. The simple answer is that most of us, most of the time are trying to solve an emotional problem by using logic as we try to create a rational solution. This is like fitting a round peg into a square hole. It simply will not work no matter how many times you try. This is because we have been told from a young age to take control of our emotions. It seems as if we are expected to just shove our emotions in a closet somewhere and shut the door. We are expected to forget that these emotions exist and we should get on with our lives. We cannot do this, it is impossible we are human beings after all.

Our primitive ancestors knew about emotions. They lived by them. Primitive man made decisions based on their instincts. If they saw a bear out in the forests they most likely ran (and most people these days would too!). If someone had food that primitive man wanted and he was hungry he may have been forced to kill for it. Faced with a situation that causes a high physiological arousal our core or primitive emotions take hold.

Imagine for a moment that you are fast asleep in your bed. You are alone in the house and you hear a noise downstairs. You think that you have imagined it and you try to go back to sleep. Then you hear someone walking up the stairs. You know that this is now very real, someone is in the house. You have a creaky stair and someone has just passed it and the stair has emitted its creaky sound. You sit up in bed and now what do you do?

- You may decide to do any of the following or perhaps something entirely different:

- You hide under the bedcovers and hope for the best.

- You grab a stick or weapon that you keep by the side of the bed.

- You leap out of bed and charge downstairs ready to confront the intruder.

- You hide in the cupboard or under the bed.

- You simply stay sitting up in bed, uncertain what to do next.

Quite often when we read about a house robbery in the comfort of our own home we are very judgemental as to how the homeowner reacted. We tend to say: well I would have done this or that differently. This is because the rational part of the brain has taken over. We are not under threat so we have time to consider what we would do given such a situation.

During times of extreme anger, fear, stress and anxiety our bodies produce a physiological response. This is known as fight or flight because we either flee a situation or we stand up and fight or face it. When we encounter such a threat a number of physiological changes occur quite rapidly in the body:

- The brain activity changes as more oxygen is sent to the limbs.

- The heart rate increases in preparation for action.

- Blood pressure increases.

- Muscles tense ready for action.

- Digestion stops or slows down.

- The mouth becomes dry.

The likelihood of encountering a significant risk to one's personal safety is fortunately remote for most of us. However, when we feel under threat or at times of significant stress we react in the same way as we would if there was intruder in our home. When we have too much work, have a deadline to meet, perhaps we have a presentation to give and we are fearful of speaking to a group of people, whenever we encounter anything that causes us to feel threatened or fearful we react in the same way that our primitive ancestors would have. This is because we have the same emotions the only difference is that we try and keep them in check. We do not show how we really feel because to lose control often has serious consequences such as the loss of your job if you become angry at your boss, the loss of liberty if you harm another human or commit a criminal act, or the loss of life if you engage in dangerous, harmful or threatening behaviour.

So, the majority of the time people tend to supress their feelings and keep them well hidden even from themselves. This aspect of modern living has serious and significant consequences. This may work for us at times but as we keep adding to the bundle of negative emotions and feelings of stress, over time we find that this weight can no longer be contained. Our feelings come to the surface and we are left to deal with the consequences.

What are the consequences? Well the answer unfortunately for many is physical or mental illness. Much of our ill health is attributed to too much stress, poor diet and lack of exercise. Aches and pains with no known cause are often common amongst individuals who dislike their jobs. Some people will be unable to see a way out of their current situation. They will feel trapped and as a consequence sink into depression. In the same way that a small child may develop tummy ache on a school day, an adult may develop aches and joint pain if the subconscious and at times the conscious mind is resisting carrying out an activity or a job that the person dislikes intensely. Begin to listen to your body; it really tries to tell you things.

Now you may be wandering what you can do about it. Well, if you feel a certain way about a job you may decide to change. Leave that job or career. Although it may sound simple often there are many other factors to be considered. At the time of writing the economy in the UK is not looking too good and for many it may be difficult to change employment easily. So what are you left with?

Well, you could do one of two things:

1. Become deeply unhappy and resentful and feel stuck in your situation.

or

2. Learn how to see things differently, possibly learn to enjoy (or at least tolerate) the situation you are presently in until you are able to move to something that you really want to do.

Now you may be asking, how can you really learn to see things differently? Well, by discovering how to be mindful and continuing to read this book!

# CHAPTER 4: MEDITATION

**An important aspect of mindfulness is meditation. Meditation has some of its origins in India where Yogis could often be seen meditating. Ancient Hindu scriptures dating back over 5,000 years also mention meditation. Buddhism and the Buddha's teaching were taken from India to Japan via China and Vietnam. It can be said, therefore, that the origins of meditation can be found in Asia. In the 1950's and 1960's Buddhism became popular in the West and the practice of meditation flourished for a while.**

Meditation is often misunderstood. Some religious practices ban their members from carrying out meditation due to a fear that a person will lose their mind or be controlled by unseen or unknown forces. There is a frequent misconception that those that meditate can be easily led, that they are vulnerable in some way. This could not be further from the truth. As you will find out for yourself shortly, meditation requires effort and discipline.

Whilst there are many people who like the IDEA of meditating and would like to feel more relaxed and calm, few apply themselves sufficiently in order to truly experience the long lasting benefits.

Why is this?

Well, there are some people who like instant results

Other people are unwilling to commit to a regular practice.

Some people lose interest.

Whilst meditation is not for everyone, a person only has to commit a few minutes each day (longer if they wish) in order to see the benefits. In the same way that we all need to spend some time taking care of our physical health we need to spend time taking care of our mind and our mental health as well. To those people who do not believe that they have the time, read on and discover the benefits of meditation. Better still begin your practice after following this section of the guide and see for yourself.

## The Benefits of Meditation

- Lower blood pressure, lower heart rate

- Reduction in stress and anxiety levels

- Clearer skin, brighter eyes

- Greater emotional stability

- A reduction in self-destructive habits and behaviour

- Improved circulation

- Inner peace

- A better understanding of oneself

Now all of these benefits of meditation are great - I bet you can't wait to get going - but hold on for a little while longer.

When I first started to meditate I went out and bought myself several CD'S which contained programmes, all of which lasted around 60 minutes or even longer. I really tried hard and after the first few days I gave up completely as I felt that I was just sitting there and not really doing anything. My mind would wander and I would think of all of the other things that I could be doing instead. I am so glad that I found other ways to learn meditation and that I am here now, typing at my computer, willing and able to share this with you. Meditation is wonderful and you simply have to learn how to do it correctly.

## The Brain

The brain is a most fascinating part of the body. The brain is made up of billions of cells called neurons. These neurons use electricity to communicate with each other. Brain activity can be measured using equipment such as an EEG machine. It is the particular combination of electrical activity that leads to one of four brain wave patterns.

**Beta:** Our brains carry out this particular brain wave pattern most of the time. This pattern occurs when you are consciously alert such as when you are at work or carrying out a complex task which requires your full attention. Your brains may also elicit this type of brainwave pattern when you feel anxious or agitated. The brainwaves occur at 13 to 60 pulses per second.

**Alpha:** These brainwaves occur when you are physically and mentally relaxed. During meditation, when carrying out a task or hobby that you enjoy, when you are reading, even as you are reading this book and when you are learning something new; these are all occasions that you emit these brain waves. Brain activity slows considerably at such times. The brain waves emit around 7 to 13 pulses per second.

**Theta:** These brain waves occur when you are at the early stages of sleep and when you are dreaming. If you have an intense emotional reaction or spiritual experience your brain will also be emitting these brainwaves. The speed of these brain waves is 4 to 7 pulses per second.

**Delta:** This is the slowest of the brain waves. These brain waves are emitted when we are asleep or unconscious. For many people this is the only time that they will emit these brain waves. However, for people who are involved in the healing arts or who practice frequent meditation these brain waves can be found when they are awake. When these brainwaves occur during sleep melatonin can be released as well as anti-ageing hormones. These waves have a very slow speed of 0.1 to 4 pulses per second. At the lower end of the scale, 0.1, a person can be considered to be brain dead.

# CHAPTER 5: MEDITATION ESSENTIALS

In order to ensure that you obtain the full benefits of your meditation there are a number of points that you have to consider:

## Decide Where to Meditate

You must find somewhere where you feel comfortable, a healing space all of your own. If you are fortunate you may have a spare room in your home that you can dedicate to such an endeavour. If this is not possible or practical for you, choose a place in your home where you will not be disturbed. Ensure that you turn off all telephones and that there are no computers or other electrical equipment nearby.

If there are other people in the house with you, ensure that you inform them of your intention to carry out meditation exercises and that you plan to do this on a daily/weekly basis. Ask them to kindly not disturb you while you are meditating. A good idea is to pop a sign on the door stating DO NOT DISTURB. Other people simply inform family members that when the door is shut they are not to be disturbed as they are meditating. Some family members are great at respecting your request for privacy, others less so.

The more that the practice of meditation becomes part of your life, the easier it will be to ignore any background noises and distractions. In addition, the more that you practice, the greater the chance that other household members will realise that you are serious about this endeavour and you will quickly be left to your own devices. Try it and see for yourself.

With regards to the room itself, set the scene for relaxation and healing by:

Using scented candles or incense.

Paint the room a relaxing colour or a combination of healing and relaxing colours. For example blue is the colour of communication, green and pink for healing and purple for spirituality. White will add light and appear to open up a small room. You might then want to add a dash of colour, or perhaps a few colourful pictures which create a feeling of relaxation such as pictures of the sea or of nature.

Remember that this is your space and your time to meditate and clear your mind of unwanted and unnecessary clutter.

## Posture and Seating

Many people think that they need to sit in a specific position in order to meditate properly. Some have been taught that they need to sit on the floor with their legs crossed in the Lotus position. This is entirely unnecessary. It is important to remember that you need to be comfortable in order to meditate. If a person wants to sit in such a position, then that's fine but it is equally as fine to sit on a chair, rug, mat or even a bean bag.

Remember to sit up reasonably straight; do not slump as your concentration and circulation will be affected. You do not need to be ram rod straight either as this is uncomfortable for most people. Keep your legs uncrossed and feet flat on the floor. That way, you are not putting any strain on your joints and you are grounded.

## Decide How Long To Meditate

As most people lead busy lives, it is important to organise your time well. Failure to do so will lead to frustration and disappointment and you will not receive the many benefits that meditation has to offer.

If you are new to meditation then begin with a few short minutes. To begin with, do not underestimate the power and benefits of even 3 minutes meditation. You may think that 3 minutes is a ridiculously short amount of time. However, stop and think again, you need to learn to control and focus your thoughts. Your mind is like a bar of slippery soap, you think that you have a grip of the task that you have set yourself and the all of a sudden your mind is elsewhere thinking of something else entirely different.

It is best to set yourself a small target to begin with and then build on that by increasing by, say a few minutes extra each week. In that way you can gradually see yourself progressing. It is a good idea not to set yourself up for failure by trying to meditate for 60 minutes then quickly becoming bored senseless and declaring that meditation is not for you.

You may wish to monitor your time by playing a track or two from a CD player to begin with. Check to see how long the track lasts and then slowly come out of your meditation in your own time at the end of it. Try not to use a clock or worse still, an alarm. If you use a clock then you will be focusing on the minutes instead of your meditation. If you use an alarm you will be quickly brought out of your nicely relaxed state, this will defeat the purpose of the session. Paying too much attention to the time is not a very mindful way to meditate!

# CHAPTER 6: BASIC MINDFULNESS MEDITATIONS

In the next few pages I have given you examples of types of meditations that you can use to begin your mindfulness training. You will learn to focus your mind and when you have finished meditating your mind will be relaxed and clear. You will begin, without effort, to focus on the moment.

Remember, if you are new to meditation begin by meditating for only a few short minutes and gradually increase the amount of time to a level that is comfortable for you and fits nicely in your schedule. Try to meditate daily or every other day in order to gain the maximum benefit. Perhaps you may wish to try all, or stick to a single style of one of the meditation techniques below. It is your choice as only you will know (with practice) which works best for you.

### Focus On an Object

Choose an object such as a plant, candle, flower or picture. Try to choose something that is connected with nature.

Close your eyes and focus inwardly.

Mentally turn down the level of any outside noise. Imagine the volume control of a radio. Turn the volume down until it can no longer be heard. See how much control you have over your senses and your environment.

Now, focus on your chosen object.

Look at the shape, texture and colour(s).

If you are looking at a picture, imagine that you have shrunk down to the size of a tiny, tiny person and you are now in the picture.

Remember to focus but also remember to blink!

When your allocated time is up, close your eyes.

Bring your attention back to your environment.

Mentally turn up the volume of the radio and become aware of the sounds around you once more.

## Focus On a Word or Mantra

During this meditation you will learn to focus on a word such as AUM. When you choose to focus in this way, all of your attention and focus is on the word itself. Your mind does not have a chance to wander so you live and focus in the moment. You also clear your mind of clutter. Try it and see for yourself:

Begin by closing your eyes for a moment.

Quiet your mind, still your thoughts.

Become aware of your body. Do you feel any tension in any areas?

If the answer is yes then focus your attention on that particular part of the body and let the tension go. If you are holding onto a lot of tension throughout your body, focus on each area in turn. Mentally say to yourself I am letting go of the tension in my neck, back, shoulders and so on until you feel that you have let that tension go.

Now, begin to say AUM. Say the word out loud or silently to yourself.

Keep the pace constant, not to fast or too slow.

The word should not sound too loud. It should appear to be in the background.

Remember, if you become distracted, bring your focus back.

When you are ready close your eyes.

End the meditation by bringing your focus back into the room and adjust to the everyday sounds all around you.

## Focus On Your Breathing

Close your eyes and listen to the sound of your breathing. Notice the nice steady rate of your breathing. Not too fast or too slow.

Now, remembering to keep your eyes closed, inhale through your nose for a count of 4.

Hold for a count of 2.

Exhale through your mouth for a count of 4.

Keep breathing in this way for the time that you have allowed yourself to meditate.

Remember, if your mind wanders, (as it most surely will at the beginning) simply re-focus your thoughts. Concentrate on your breathing and nothing else.

When you have finished keep your eyes closed and return your breathing to normal.

Slowly, slowly bring your focus back in to the room and open your eyes when you are ready.

## Focus On Visualisation

Most people can visualise. If I ask you to think about a close friend or family member I bet you can picture them quite easily. The key to being good at this exercise is to picture something that you are drawn to, something that you like or even somewhere you would like to go.

Begin by choosing what you are going to visualise. This might be a tropical island, a snow capped mountain or a meadow with a lake or a stream running through it.

Now close your eyes and see yourself in this special place.

In your mind, have a good look around.

You may hear the waves of the sea, feel the sun on your back or hear the snow crunching beneath your feet as you walk beneath the snowy mountains.

In your mind, turn up the colour of the picture.

In your imagination your picture should now be very bright.

Focus on what you see.

Once again, if your mind wanders, and it will at first, bring your focus back to where it should be.

When you are ready, in your mind, take yourself for a walk.

Focus on each step.

Become mindful of each step.

When your allocated time is up, release any visual imagery and very gradually bring your attention back into the room.

# CHAPTER 7: TIME FOR ACTION

**Note:** *When reading the following chapters, try to carry out the activities as described. All too often people read books and think that the subject matter was interesting. At times people may also think that they would like to try to carry out an exercise, recipe or even visit a place that has been mentioned in the book or article. All too often, once the book is read, the idea and good intentions are now placed in the back of the mind. Other tasks and more pressing issues have taken the persons attention away from the book and the desire to move forward has fizzled away. If you really want to change how you think and feel* ***JUST DO IT.*** *Become a Mindful person for the rest of your life by following the simple instructions and carrying out the exercises. Be consistent, be thorough and most importantly of all, be honest with yourself. It really is that simple. Begin now.*

## How do you feel today?

Many people would answer that by replying in a manner that is considered socially acceptable. The reply might be "fine thanks" or "I'm good", or "very well thank you" or one of a multitude of other socially acceptable responses. This response may not be how the person is really feeling.

We tend to keep aspects of how we feel hidden. This is not always a bad thing. After all, if you feel very angry with someone you may have to control your anger to prevent a physical attack and possible time in prison.

The way we feel often has nothing to do with the now, the present. Let me explain this a little more. If we see someone who we don't especially like, perhaps it is someone who has been rude to us in the past, we feel a certain way. We may feel agitated, we may try to avoid them or we may even run through a number of quick replies to questions that this person may ask.

We do this, you see, because our mind has linked up the current situation with a past one (or a number of them). Our brains are like computers and look for the "best fit" when we process what we see. Our brain receives so much information all of the time that it catalogues what is sees and only information which is perceived as threatening or of importance is given attention. This was an ideal way of living for our ancestors. They would see a threat and the fight or flight response would kick in. Now, most of the time, we live our lives in a kind of daze. We walk around thinking of things in the past and planning for the future.

Going back to the idea that you have just seen someone that you do not like, imagine now that they have approached you and smiled. The person is ultra-friendly and polite and the conversation goes smoothly. After a short while you both go your separate ways.

Now, what are you thinking?

I bet your first thought is that there must be a reason why the person is being so polite. Do they want something? Do they have an ulterior motive? You see, your mind is very reluctant to let go of thought patterns that it has made. The more you know somebody or carry out an activity the stronger the neural pathways become. This is why most of us most of the time live in a daze. We get up and go to work. We take the same route to work and we do the same things day in and day out until we are told that we can stop. We can retire or perhaps we die and many of us do not even know that we have only lived a fraction of our lives and little of our potential has been achieved.

It does not have to be this way. Not anymore. You may feel a little scared now or even angry as you realise that the words you have read are the truth. Remember now, and in the future that anger has no place in the present. Your feelings of anger (or anything else) that you feel which is not directly happening now are simply an illusion. They are related to something that has already happened to you in the past and this is what you cannot change.

By increasing your awareness of how you feel now you will learn, with practice to become aware of and accept any feelings for what they are and you will learn, again with practice to let go. Now this is not always as easy to do as it may seem and the reason that you may be feeling a particular emotion may be deeply embedded in a traumatic even in the past. If this is you, if something has happened to you in the past and you feel very, very strong emotions try to remember that by holding onto the emotions you are only hurting yourself. You are not hurting the other people or person who has harmed you. If this is your situation, you may feel the need to seek professional therapy and I would urge you to do so. This book is not intended as a substitute for any therapy or medical intervention.

Mindfulness is concerned with:

- How you behave.

- How you think.

- How you feel.

All three are inter-related; they do not flow in a particular order and any one aspect can change the other. So, for example, if you are going to an interview you may feel nervous and you may think that your mind will go blank and you will make a fool of yourself. Outwardly you may appear to be confident. On the other hand you may feel confident and the questions that are asked may cause you to stumble over the words, your mind goes blank and you begin to tremble.

What we see or perceive of another person or situation is not always how that person feels or really is deep at their core, their soul. It would be a good idea if you could remember that, as even by remembering this small piece of advice may lead you to be more thoughtful with the words you use and what you think when around other people. By thinking in this way you will be less quick to react, less critical .Slowing down your thoughts allows you to give a true and appropriate response based on the now and not a response which is based on an almost reflex reaction.

When we meet a person for the first time we pay attention to them completely. We observe their behaviour, pay attention to their words. We look at how they dress and conduct themselves. From now on, whenever you meet or interact with someone give them your full attention. It does not matter if you already know them or if you are meeting them for the first time or even if that person is the ticket inspector on the train.

I have recently noticed that all too often people in the service sector are not really paid attention to. I was in a store recently and the person in front of me bought a variety of goods, paid little attention to the store assistant and none or little eye contact was made. The assistant responded in a similar way. When it was my turn to be served, I made a conscious decision to thoroughly engage with the assistant. I smiled, made eye contact and received a similar response. I felt good after making human contact and I am sure the sales assistant felt the same way. The next time you are buying goods in a store try this little exercise out and note how you feel. I can almost guarantee that you will feel a little joy in your heart.

Below I have written a body scan meditation. You can do this meditation/exercise any time you choose. It will help increase your awareness of how you really feel at any particular time. It will help you slow down and focus on the moment, the here and now. Try it and see for yourself.

## Body Scan Meditation

As with the other meditations, find a quiet place where you will not be disturbed, if at all possible.

If you are carrying out this meditation whist you are at work or somewhere else which may be busy or perhaps you are unable to find a quiet place, simply allow your mind to be still and focus internally. With practice you will be able to do this and it does become easier the more that you meditate.

**Now begin:**

Imagine a light, like a spotlight starting at the top of your head.

The light is warm and comforting.

Now see and feel the light move down over the head.

Pay attention to how you feel. When any emotion comes to the surface just simply notice it and allow it to drift way.

Imagine that you are simply an observer, note the emotion and let it go. If it helps, feel and see the emotion drift way, gently, gently further and further away on a big white cloud.

Now imagine the light move over to the heart area. Again notice and observe any emotions that arise from this. Allow the emotions to pass.

Now see the light really expand.

See and feel the light expand so that your whole body is in a large golden or white bubble of protective, nurturing light.

Again, allow any emotions to come to the surface. Allow them to do this and simply observe them, do not try to analyse them and do not be critical of them. In your own time, allow the emotions to drift away.

When you become aware that there are no further emotions that are going to surface at this particular time enjoy the stillness and peace that is all around you.

Allow the light to fade away and bring your attention to the present.

> **Note:** *If carrying out this exercise in a busy environment you can simply imagine, with your eyes open, that the emotions are surfacing when focusing on the head and the heart areas. In your mind, you can allow those emotions to drift away and you will be left feeling calm and relaxed.*

## Mindfulness: Key Points

- Begin to pay attention to everything that you do as if you are doing it for the first time.

- Slow down and think and be less critical.

- Be aware of your thoughts, accept your feelings and let them go.

- How you feel now should be based on what is happening at this moment in time and not something that has happened in the past, or something that may happen in the future.

- Carry out the body scan meditation so that you can let go of your emotions.

# CHAPTER 8: YOUR PRECIOUS 24 HOURS

## A WHOLE DAY TO LIVE

**E**ach morning most of us are given a present: twenty four hours for you to live your life. Most of us do not realise, or take the time to consider, that we have this precious gift. Why is it that, for many of us, it is only when we are sick or dying that we realise what we had? If a doctor informs a patient that they only have a short time to live, they may accomplish more, find their life purpose and do what they really want to do in the time that they have left, than they had achieved in many years of living on this earth.

When you are grateful for what you have, when you are grateful for each precious moment and you really look at the world around you, then you are living in the moment.

When people go on holiday and arrive at their chosen destination they take the time to look at what is around them. For many, going on holiday is the only time during the year that they feel truly alive. I think that this is very sad. Out of three hundred and sixty five days some people only feel alive for perhaps fourteen days. So, the question to be asked now is: what is life like the rest of the time and how can the way you think and see the world around you be changed so that you feel alive all, or at least most, of the time?

Imagine that it is Monday morning and the alarm goes off for you to get up and go to work; what is your first thought? Is it: "oh well, another week of work where I hate my job/my boss/my work/my life. How did I get myself into this situation?" Do you then stumble out of bed, rush to the bathroom stubbing your toe in your haste as you are now late, having stayed in bed for too long and now you know that if you do not move really fast you will hit the rush hour traffic and be late for work.

Or perhaps your first thoughts are these instead:

As your alarm goes off you slowly wake up and you realise that you have another twenty four hours to live. You know in your heart that you are lucky to be alive. Your mind is drawn to the day ahead and you run through your day and what your expectations of it are in your mind. You also briefly ponder on any difficult aspects to your day and you realise that you are mentally prepared for them. With your thoughts in order you slowly get out of bed and make your way to the bathroom.

Try to be mindful in everything that you do.

When taking a shower be grateful that you have running water. Remind yourself that many people in the world still do not have access to clean, clear fresh water and sanitation. I remember when I was very young, we did not have an indoor toilet at home I used to really hate going outside when it was dark or cold in order to use the toilet. On the odd occasion there was a spider or even a mouse in the toilet and I would then race to my parents screaming for them to get the offending creature removed from the toilet. When we had an indoor toilet I thought that we were living in luxury. I thought that it was wonderful to be able to use it anytime of the day or night and be in relative warmth.

As you wash yourself imagine that you are also cleansing away any negative thoughts and feelings. You are about to begin your day totally fresh without any feelings of anger or worry or any other negative and destructive feelings. Remember now, that even though you have some structure to you day, you should not have any expectations as to how you will think and feel. This is because your thoughts and feelings will change second by second as you interact with others and as you truly observe your environment.

When you get dressed be grateful for the clothes that you have. Feel the texture of the fabric and concentrate on what you are doing as you do up buttons, zips and belts. When you put your shoes on imagine what it would be like not to have shoes. How cut and damaged your feet would be and how much they would hurt without shoes.

When you eat your breakfast, and yes, I get the feeling that not everyone does have breakfast. Please remember that you would not expect your car to run without fuel so why would you even think that you do not need to eat and provide yourself with some of the essential nutrients at the start of the day?

Remember that time is not an excuse. Do not fool yourself by saying that you do not have enough time. If you do not make time in order to have breakfast then your blood sugar will be low. You may be grumpy and irritable and not really know why and this may go on for many years. Think of the hours of your life you have wasted all because you have had low blood sugar. What a waste!

Anyway, as you eat breakfast feel grateful for the food on your plate. As you eat, really chew your food and concentrate on the texture of it. Chew thoroughly and imagine, as you swallow each mouthful, that you are gently nourishing your body and taking care of it. When you eat in this way you are being mindful of what you are doing. When you eat in this way you will not be inclined to over eat and you will become satisfied more quickly and easily.

Do not eat during moments of anger or when you are arguing. The food will not taste the same and it may stick in your throat. You may also over indulge because you are not feeding a hunger for food but an emotional hunger instead. Do not engage in distractions. Do not listen to the news, read a newspaper or watch TV at this time. By the very nature of the news, you will watch, hear or read sad or even heart breaking information. This will be a distraction from what you are doing, eating your breakfast. If you want news, make time for it when you can give it your full attention.

When I was a child, during meal times my father used to eat very quickly. My father had been a prisoner of war in Siberia and had been given mostly chunks of stale bread to eat and he had found that if he did not eat his bread quickly enough or if he did not hide it in a very safe place for later when he would be even more hungry, then that food would be taken away from him. It was because of this that my father ate quickly and because of this that he was grateful for the food that we had. He could never understand why people would punish themselves by going on weird diets or starving themselves when most of us in the West are fortunate to have all of the food that we need.

## Your Journey

Each time you step out of your door you are going from one place to another. You are closing one door and opening another. When you open another door, when you step out into the world your journey begins. It is up to you. You can carry out this journey in a Mindful way or you can carry out the journey without really seeing what is all around you. There is beauty, even if you live in a less than desirable area.

Whenever you begin a journey, with each step that you take you are imprinting on the earth. Your imprint, your shadow, can leave behind good and not so good impressions on the earth. When you are walking be grateful for walking. If you have ever had a leg injury, a fracture or painful injury then you know how important each step is, how much each step counts. Often when we see someone who is struggling to walk we may feel sorry for them. The truth is that the person struggling may be getting much more out of walking that the more able person ever will. Each step in the struggle is an achievement. How often do most of us feel a sense of achievement through such a simple task as walking?

As you walk look at what is around you. Pay attention to any flower or bird that catches your eye and be grateful for having the gift of sight and the eyes to see. If you live in a deprived area then there is still much beauty to be seen. You may delight in the smile or laugh of a small child and even the beauty of the intensity of colour of a wildflower. This is your neighbourhood and you now feel part of it. You are connecting, living in the moment. You may see people scurrying past with a frown on their face, deep in thought but you know that they are not really thinking of what they are doing. They are focused on the past or the future.

As you walk remember to breathe deeply. As you fill your lungs with air imagine that you are nourishing your body with this essential life force. Be grateful for your ability to breath, it is essential to life after all!

If your journey involves driving or using public transport then there are many ways to be mindful on your journey. If you are driving, be grateful for the car or any other form of transport that you have. Be observant of the people on the road and be respectful and polite. If you feel that you must race to your destination why is this? Why are you racing through life? If your first response to this is that you are racing because you are late then are you taking on too much? Is your mind wandering and not staying on task so that when you come back to the present you realise that you have little time to get done what is needed. When you drive fast the reactions in your body speed up and you become hyper alert. This is almost like a fight or flight response. If this occurs on a regular basis you may develop health problems and increase your levels of stress and anxiety. All of this seems a big price to pay for not paying attention to the here and now and not living in the moment.

If you are using public transport do not become annoyed if the transport is late. Instead, look around you and become mindful or your environment. I have often engaged in conversation and exchanged pleasant words with fellow travellers whilst waiting for a bus or train.

Remember that a few kind words can brighten a person's day. This is especially so if the person is elderly as here in the West all too often the elderly may be lonely and live alone without the support of family or friends. Imagine how much you can brighten up someone else's day by being mindful and paying attention to them. What a lovely gift that is and it only costs you a few minutes of your time.

During your day focus on each task at hand. If you are at work and you enjoy your work then really be grateful for having a job that you enjoy. If you do not like your job then focus on your work because if you allow your mind to wander too much the day will seem longer and you will become more frustrated and everything will seem much more difficult. Be grateful for the little things: someone offering to make you a drink or help with a problem, a kind word from a manager. Be mindful of other people and be willing to offer them a gift too. A smile or a joke with a colleague also makes the day go by pleasantly. Offer to take work or a willingness to help someone struggling with too much work. When we help others we are living in the present. When we interact with others we are able to put aside our own sometimes negative thoughts as we live in the present.

## Peter's Story

Peter had developed severe rheumatoid arthritis in multiple joints. Medication seemed to have little effect and Peter slowly became more and more withdrawn as the pain took hold. He found that he spent most of his time focusing on his pain and as a result he became grumpy and quite miserable. His relationships were also affected both at work and at home.

One day Peter became involved in a disagreement with a colleague. During the disagreement the colleague stated that Peter had changed and that he his life was focused on his condition. Peter, once he had cooled down and released his anger, found that what his colleague had said was true. Peter's life had been so focused on his pain that he had given up all of his hobbies and he had become totally insular.

Peter then began to think about other ways that his condition could be treated; he tried acupuncture and this was most effective. A friend recommended a meditation class which, to his surprise he found that he quite enjoyed. Peter said that he thought that he had been feeding his pain by focusing on it.

With the combination of acupuncture and meditation Peter found that over time he was able to reduce the intensity of his pain and discomfort and on some days he felt little or no pain at all. Peter found that when he was absorbed and focused on what he was doing he would hardly notice the pain at all. He also began to become more involved with his local community by carrying out charity work.

Peter opened his eyes to those in need around him and he became grateful for what he had. At times he even became grateful when he felt pain because the pain, he noticed, often developed now only when he was over tired so Peter saw this as his body's way of telling him to stop doing something or to slow down. Peter said that he felt that he was really living now and that the meditations in particular helped him to feel as if he had some control over his mind, something that he had never experienced before.

As you go about your day become aware of the people around you. Being kind to other people will bring kindness back to you. Hold the door open for someone to walk through, offer your seat to a person in greater need on a bus or train. These small acts of kindness go quite a way to helping you feel good inside as well as imprinting positive vibrations in the air and on the earth.

When you arrive home for the evening you need time to relax and it is important to do so. If you are fortunate enough to share your home with loved ones and you are asked about your day do not spend too much time talking about the negative things that have happened. You are unable to change the past and the negative words spoken will change the vibrations and energy in the home which may cause tension for all around you.

When you eat your evening meal, be grateful for the food on your plate. I am sure many of you would have been told to clear your plate when you were young as children in Asia/Africa or somewhere else are starving and would be grateful for the food that you had. Whilst our parents and caregivers had said this to us in order to encourage us to eat, most of us, thank goodness, really did not and, even now as adults, do not understand what it was like to be hungry. For this we should be grateful.

When we choose our food we should eat food which is as natural and as fresh as possible. This is because we should strive to be at one with nature and of course so that we obtain optimum nutrition. When you eat remember to chew your food thoroughly and avoid any harsh or negative words (if possible). Remember to avoid distractions such as the TV , reading a book, newspaper or papers from work. When you eat only eat and the chances are that you will not over indulge.

The evening is for many, one of the best times of the day for meditation. Take your time to relax and breathe properly and unwind, especially if you have had a stressful day. Remember your time to meditate and focus your mind is your way of showing your appreciation for the gift of a healthy functioning mind, truly something to be grateful for.

# CHAPTER 9: NEGATIVE THOUGHTS & FEELINGS

As we go about our day we may experience many thoughts and feelings. Most of our thoughts, if we are lucky, are pleasant or neutral. Now and then life also presents us with challenges and obstacles. This is when we experience unpleasant thoughts. People often ask how they can learn to deal with difficult times and unpleasant thoughts in a Mindful and thoughtful way.

Our feelings help to control our thoughts and actions. If someone says or does something to us that we do not like we feel uncomfortable; as a result of this, all too often, our first reaction is to strike back verbally or physically. This may be because we have been hurt in some way; we want to hurt the other person because we have been wounded by their words or actions. There may be an element of truth in what the person has said or done.

When we feel injured in this way our whole body reacts. We feel tense, our heart rate speeds up and our breathing becomes shallow. We have a fight or flight response and this is why some people do physically lash out when angry or hurt. Other people become withdrawn, they simply want to curl up in a ball and be left alone.

## Take Back Control

When we encounter such a difficult situation our first focus must be internal. This is why meditation is so important; we must begin by taking back control of our emotions. How is this done? We can do this by breathing; as we breathe in and out in a slow and controlled way we can say to ourselves one simple word: "relax". As we do so we quickly feel that we have begun to relax. Once we begin to feel more relaxed we feel more in control, more like our usual selves and our emotions begin to return to their usual state. Once we begin to feel more in control we lose any fear that we have been experiencing and we can think in a more rational way.

## Identify Your Emotions

Now we must take the time to recognise our emotions. Ask yourself: "what am I feeling?" Make friends with your feelings by accepting that they are part of you. This may be difficult at first as many of us are used to hiding our feelings from ourselves. We may practice self-deceit and denial to avoid facing what we truly feel. You and your feelings cannot be separated, you are your feelings and your feelings are part of you. It is impossible to deny any aspect of yourself for very long, if you do so you will find that those negative feelings will develop and grow with time. It is like watching a plant grow. The difference is that as a plant grows into a beautiful product of nature, your negative feelings that you have denied will manifest as an ugly and powerful shadow.

Always present but often in the background ready to manifest at an opportune moment.

When observing your feelings it may be beneficial to imagine your feelings are floating on clouds. Simply observe them and let them float right past you. Try not to judge, just accept what is coming into your mind. If you feel anger, hate, jealousy do not be worried about those feelings. Simply observe and let them pass.

## Let Go

Now that you have identified your feelings you must learn to let go. A good way of going this is to simply say that you are letting go of each emotion in turn. You can let go of all of your anger, hurt, hate or fear in this way.

When I do this exercise, as I mentioned previously, I imagine the emotion sitting on a cloud and I mentally push it far, far away from my body. If the emotion is very deep this exercise may require some practice. Ask yourself what you have to gain by holding on to the emotion. If it is your mistaken belief that you are hurting another person by holding on to an emotion think again; the only person you are hurting is you! The emotion will begin to eat you up inside and you may become ill from holding on to all of that negativity.

Sadly for many people they find it difficult to release such an emotion and this is because the emotion has become part of their lives and by letting it go there is not very much left. It is like someone who fights for justice after something has happened to them. Once justice has been obtained the person still cannot let go because all of their energy has been focussed on obtaining justice.

Many people act in the same way with their work. They have specific emotions attached to the job but when the job is no longer there through retirement, or perhaps they have been made redundant, there is little left of the person because the emotion has gone and they feel that part of them is missing. In order to truly free yourself you must be prepared to become your own therapist.

## Moving Forward

When you are successfully able to let go of an emotion you need to be able to sit down and assess your life. Again, do this in a Mindful way. Simply acknowledge any thoughts that come into your mind and let them pass.

With time and practice those thoughts that are important to you will keep returning. You will see patterns emerging. You will find how easy it is for good and positive thoughts to enter your mind. At this stage, after you have practiced this exercise daily for several minutes or more over a period of a week or so, you will find that you have the information available to you to make the changes necessary in order to become whole once again. You will find an interest or a hobby which will enable you to fill the gap where the negative aspect had resided.

This aspect of mindfulness is very similar to therapy as it works in very much the same way. A person present with what they perceive is a problem which is causing them distress in some aspect of their lives. It is only when the person can look within, to themselves that they are able to find the solution. Often this requires an acceptance of an aspect of themselves that they do not like. Once this part of themselves is acknowledged they can finally let go and be themselves.

When we are mindful we are only interested in our own thoughts, emotions and behaviour. We should not try to analyse another person's actions or intent because we never really know the reasons they have for doing so. If we judge or try to analyse, we are only placing our own interpretation of another person's actions and we do this through our own eyes and not theirs.

# CHAPTER 10: MINDFULNESS: KEY POINTS

- Focus completely on each and every activity.

- Learn to take control of your mind and do not allow it to go back forth from one thing to the next.

- Carry out meditation on a regular basis as this is essential for a healthy mind.

- When walking observe all that is around you like you are seeing it for the first time.

- Be responsible for you own thoughts, words and actions.

- Do not judge or be critical of others or their behaviour.

- Be kind and considerate to others.

- Do not harm other people, animals or any other living thing.

# ALSO BY MARION MCGEOUGH:

If you have enjoyed reading this book about Mindfulness you may also be interested in other books by Marion McGeough:

**Shoden: The definitive guide to first degree Reiki: Mindfulness, Meditation, Reiki treatments and more.**

**A Beginner's Guide to the Chakras.**

**Crystal Healing and the Human Energy Field: A Beginners Guide**

Hypnosis CD:
**Overcome Your Fear of Flying**

All products available from Amazon